T0014940

WOULD YOU RATHER? ANCIENT GREEKS

First published in Great Britain 2024 by Red Shed, part of Farshore

An imprint of HarperCollins*Publishers*
1 London Bridge Street, London SE1 9GF
www.farshore.co.uk

HarperCollins*Publishers*
Macken House, 39/40 Mayor Street Upper,
Dublin 1, D01 C9W8

Red Shed is a registered trademark of HarperCollins*Publishers* Ltd.

Written by Clive Gifford
Illustrated by Tim Wesson
Copyright © HarperCollins*Publishers* Limited 2024

ISBN 978 0 00 859931 7
Printed and bound in the UK using 100% Renewable Electricity at CPI Group (UK) Ltd.
001

A CIP catalogue record for this title is available from the British Library.

MIX
Paper | Supporting
responsible forestry
FSC™ C007454

This book contains FSC™ certified paper and other controlled
sources to ensure responsible forest management.

For more information visit: www.harpercollins.co.uk/green

CLIVE GIFFORD • TIM WESSON

WOULD YOU RATHER? ANCIENT GREEKS

RED
SHED

Contents

Introduction

Hello – or **Χαίρετε**, as they said in ancient Greek! Welcome to the amazing, surprising and fascinating world of ancient Greece, a civilization that packed in a LOT. The ancient Greeks invented catapults, cheesecake (yum), theatre, the Olympics, showers and the yo-yo – and that's not all. The Greeks were BIG thinkers and made developments in philosophy, maths and engineering, and created systems we still use today, like democracy and trials by jury.

This book is packed with facts, fun challenges and mind-boggling 'would you rather' questions that will take you way back in time, to see what life was *really* like in ancient Greece.

Are you ready?

Ancient Greece

How it all started

There have been people in the area we know today as Greece for thousands of years. The Minoan civilization got going on the island of Crete around a whopping 4,000 years ago, and the Mycenaean Greeks were there until the 1400sBCE. But it wasn't until around 800BCE that the ancient Greeks we know and love began to flourish.

Greece wasn't one big empire, like the Roman Empire, or a single kingdom like ancient Egypt. Instead, the ancient Greek world was made up of lots of smaller city-states spread around the mainland and islands of Greece and beyond, such as Athens, Sparta and Olympia. They didn't always get on, and wars kept their armies and navies nice and busy.

For a few centuries, ancient Greece was THE place to be. It had grand temples and palaces, poetry, and powerful military forces. Super-bright minds flocked to the region and pushed knowledge forward.

So, grab your sandals and let's get going . . .

WOULD YOU RATHER

practice your skills as a top Olympic athlete

OR plot and scheme as a Greek ruler?

AHH, FAME AND FORTUNE, MONEY, SUCCESS, LISTENING TO ADORING FANS CHANTING YOUR NAME... WAIT, ARE THEY FANS, OR AN ANGRY MOB? BEING A BIG NAME IN ANCIENT GREECE DEFINITELY HAD ITS PERKS, BUT NOT EVERYONE WAS FAMOUS FOR GOOD, HONEST REASONS...

Be a famous Olympic athlete

Are you a whizz on the sports field? Whether it's high jump, football or running that you love, you've made a good choice!

You may have watched the Olympic Games on TV – but did you know they started in 776BCE, in ancient Greece? They were originally part of a festival at Olympia to honour the god Zeus.

Wish I'd entered the javelin instead...

The Olympics became the biggest sporting event in the ancient world and ran for almost 1,000 years– and most athletes who took part were nude.*

For the first 52 years, there was only one event, a running race called the *stade* (about 190m long).

Over the years, more events were added including chariot racing, boxing, the long jump, discus, javelin and the brutal *pankration* (see page 102 – not for the squeamish). The games were held

*Except those who took part in the *hoplitodromos* race. They wore a helmet, leg guards and a heavy shield, like a hoplite soldier (see page 64).

once every four years, just as they are today, and different city-states would compete against each other. From the ninth century BCE, a truce was made, stopping any wars, so athletes and spectators could travel safely.

Competitors had to swear an oath that they would compete fairly, while standing in front of a terrifying statue of Zeus, with their hand on a slice of raw wild boar flesh.

If you won, all you'd get – officially, at least – was a crown of woven olive leaves called *kotinos*. But don't fret – far bigger rewards awaited you back home, as winning was a great source of pride. You might be given money or property by your grateful city, or be allowed not to pay taxes. Some Olympic champions from Athens were given free meals for life!

Some winners wanted it all and used their sporting fame as a springboard to a career in politics. Take Gelon of Syracuse, the 488BCE chariot racing champ. Three years after his Olympic victory, he was crowned ruler of his city-state. Win-win!

Be a famous Greek ruler

Have you got a brain full of cunning plans? Not bothered by what other people think? If your answer's yes, you might make a successful ancient Greek tyrant!

Each Greek city-state was run differently – some had a king in charge, others were ruled by one powerful family (or several). Athens, for a time, was a democracy – lots of people had a say.*

Sometimes, though, a single figure, called a tyrant, would boldly sweep in with an army, seize power and become sole ruler.

...And stay out!

Taking power was one thing – keeping it was the next challenge. As a newbie tyrant, you'd need to keep the army on your side to protect you. And ruling wasn't as easy as it looked. If you bumped off a well-liked figure, fought an unpopular war, or introduced harsh laws or taxes, you couldn't expect to be a tyrant for long.

Some ancient Greeks were so famous and successful that they have gone down in history and are still known today - turn to page 78 for more . . .

* Well, lots of men. Women, slaves and foreigners couldn't join in.

GREEK EXTRAS
Slaves, helots and metics

Ancient Greek society had different classes of people. At the top were citizens and at the bottom were slaves. Other groups were in between. They may have had better lives than slaves, but that wasn't saying much!

Slaves

Slaves were a must for every well-off Greek household. There were as many slaves as there were citizens in some Greek cities.

You might become a slave if you were captured during wartime or by deadly slave traders who invaded your homelands, bound you up in chains, and sailed you to Greece. There, slaves could be bought, sold and even rented, maybe for a day, week or year.

As a slave, your owners would feed you a bit but you received no pay and couldn't own property. In fact, you had next to no rights. You could be passed on as a gift to another person, and it wasn't a crime for your owner to thump or whip you whenever they liked.

Metics

Many Greek city-states were home to metics, who were free citizens who had moved from elsewhere. (You wouldn't have to travel far to be counted as a metic – some moved a short distance to a neighbouring city-state.)

In Athens, metics made mega contributions, helping it grow into the biggest of the Greek city-states. But did the citizens thank them? Nope! Metics weren't allowed to vote or own land. They also had to pay for the privilege of living in the city-state. They were

How much???

charged an extra tax called the *metoikion* each year. This was equal to about one or two day's wages, and if you refused to pay, you could be made a slave. *Ouch!*

Helots

In Sparta, there was a whole different class – the helots. They were a bit like slaves in that they worked as farm labourers, giving their Spartan master a chunk of what they produced. However, they were owned by the state, so couldn't be sold by individuals.

The helots outnumbered the Spartans, and kept them feeling *really* on edge. Helot rebellions caused BIG problems for Sparta, and it developed a military focus partly to keep the helots under their control.

WOULD YOU RATHER

see a play at an ancient Greek theatre

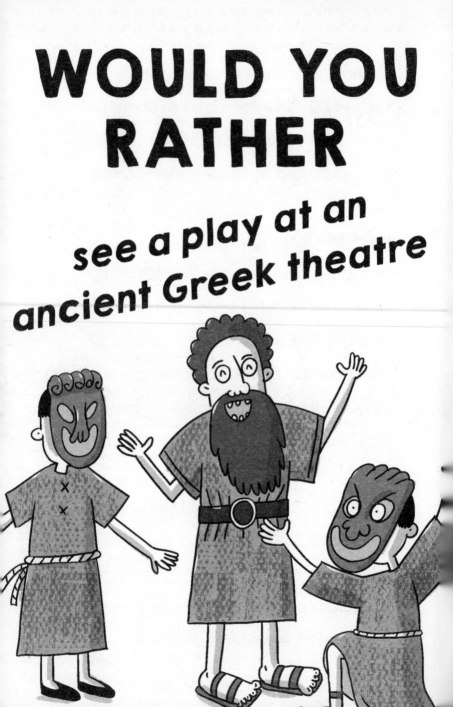

OR take part in a fun-filled festival?

GOOD NEWS, YOU'VE GOT THE DAY OFF, YOU LUCKY THING! THE ANCIENT GREEK WORLD IS YOUR OYSTER ... WHAT DO YOU FANCY DOING? THERE WERE NO TELEVISIONS, SMART PHONES OR COMPUTER GAMES, BUT THERE WERE THE WORLD'S FIRST PLAYS. AND IF YOU'RE NOT A THEATRE FAN, YOU COULD ALWAYS GO TO A FESTIVAL TO KEEP YOURSELF AMUSED ...

Go to see a play

Find a seat and get comfortable – the play's about to start!

The ancient Greeks first watched plays performed at the bottom of sloping hills. These locations were called *theatron*, meaning, 'the watching place'. Perfect. This purpose-built theatre had a semi-circular stage called an *orchestra*, surrounded by a series of semi-circular stone steps for people to sit on. It also had a *skené*, a backdrop that actors could use as an offstage area. Theatres at Ephesus and Argos were so large they could hold around 20,000 spectators!

As a theatre-goer, you'd need plenty of stamina (and snacks). Plays could last *all day*.

Officials would wander through the audience holding stout wooden canes, used to give a whack to any audience member who wasn't behaving themselves. No heckling!

Onstage, all the actors and performers were men (bad luck, Greek girls), and most were singers and dancers in a group called the chorus. Acting was pretty easy in ancient Greece as actors used face masks which had exaggerated expressions carved and painted on them. Some were double-sided, so they could flip from happy to angry or sad in an instant.

Plays were sometimes comedies about everyday life, sometimes serious tragedies packed with misfortune and death. Famous writers of tragedy, such as Euripides, Aeschylus and Sophocles, wrote on scrolls made from pressed river reeds. As well as being a champion playwright, Euripides was also a pioneer. He often used a crane in his work that could hoist actors up and down – useful when the plays included gods, who would swoop in and out of the action.

Go to a festival

Ancient Greek festivals weren't like today's music festivals. No huge stages, famous bands or stalls selling burgers and silly hats. Festivals were held to celebrate or honour the ancient Greek gods (see page 34). And with many gods, came many festivals – Athens had around 120 festival days every year. Most festivals involved sacrifices to the gods – watch out, farm animals. For humans, though, there would be singing, dancing, parades and plenty of grub. Party central! Here are a few big ancient Greek festivals:

Anthesteria

This three-day party was held in Athens in early spring, and honoured the god of wine-making and partying, Dionysus. It included a lot of wine-drinking contests! People smeared tar on their doors and chewed leaves of certain trees to keep the souls of the dead from attacking them. Creepy!

Hybristica

This festival was held in the city-state of Argos, in honour of the goddess Aphrodite. It saw men and women swap clothes and roles. Women could finally treat men as inferior and order them around. About time!

Carneia

Spartans really loved their fitness – so, of course, they turned their festivals into exercise. Their Carneia festival saw a group of boys chase a man wearing garlands of flowers. If the boys caught him, it was thought to bring good luck.

Thesmophoria

Women weren't allowed at all festivals –
but they did sometimes hold their own.
The autumn festival of Thesmophoria
honoured the goddess of farming and
fertility, Demeter, and her daughter,
Persephone, and was only celebrated by
women. Pigs were sacrificed and thrown
into deep pits called *megara*. Once the
meat was rotten, women would retrieve
it and place it on an altar. The remains
were then scattered along with seeds on
the fields – it was thought they would
ensure a good harvest.

**Phew, that's a lot of celebrating!
A lot of Greek plays and festivals
were all about gods and mythology.
To meet some more mythological
figures, turn the page . . .**

Greek gods hall of fame

The ancient Greeks had several generations of gods – the most famous were the Olympians, named because they lived on Mount Olympus. Each of them had their own interests – such as the sea, the moon, or hunting. They were also happy to get involved in the lives of humans – whether people asked for it or not.

Here are just a few of the top gods. Once you've met them all, it's time to decide – which god's temple would you rather visit?

Zeus

The Big Cheese amongst the
Olympians. Zeus controlled the Sun,
lightning and thunder, and often carried
a thunderbolt in one hand. He was
hot-headed at times, and many Greeks
believed his temper affected the weather.

Zeus led the Olympians into battle
against the Titans (a different generation
of gods) and was said to be protector
of cities and property. He also kept
strangers and guests from harm.

In case you think Zeus was all good,
let's make it clear – he wasn't. He could
be cruel, like the time he got annoyed

at a character called Prometheus for giving humans the gift of fire. Zeus' punishment was to chain Prometheus to a rock where eagles ate his liver. Ouch. He also had many girlfriends, which made his wife, Hera, extremely cross.

Poseidon

This god of horses, seas and oceans was easily recognized as he always carried a three-pronged fork – and it wasn't for eating his dinner. It was called a trident, and when he struck the ground he could make earthquakes – powerful stuff!

And that's not all. Like Zeus, he could

easily lose his temper. If he blew his top, so did the seas – *wave* hello to some huge thunderstorms!

Amongst Poseidon's children were a one-eyed giant called Cyclops, the god Triton who was half-man, half-fish, and a sea monster called Charybdis, who created giant whirlpools that could suck entire ships underwater!

Athena

This daughter of Zeus was the goddess of wisdom and tactics in battles. Athena liked to be crafty in other ways, too – she was also the goddess of weaving and pottery.

Although she could be kind and wise, Athena sometimes got vengeful –

such as when she lost a weaving contest against a skilful woman called Arachne and turned her into a spider.

Athena had some pretty intense rivalries with other gods, including

Poseidon. According to legend, both of them wanted to become god of the same Greek city, so they had a competition. Whoever brought the city-dwellers the best gift would win. Poseidon gave the city a spring of water. Sounds useful, right? Not so fast . . . Being the god of the sea, he'd made a salty seawater spring, which was impossible to drink from. *Yuck*! Epic fail, Poseidon.

Athena's gift was far more valuable: the first olive tree. Its wood could be used to build houses and tools, its leaves provided shade, and its fruits could be eaten or pressed to make olive oil. Her victory meant the city was named . . . Athens!

Hestia

Peaceful Hestia was goddess of homes, families and the hearth (a fireplace used for cooking). It was said that the crackling of the fire was Hestia's laughter – though no one's sure what the joke was.

Hestia was nowhere near as loud, hot-headed or boastful as most of the other Greek gods – she kept out of their arguments, and rejected Poseidon and Apollo who both wanted to marry her.

Every Greek city had at least one temple or shrine dedicated to Hestia. In it, a fire would be lit in her honour and never allowed to go out.

Hermes

The god Hermes was a laugh a minute – providing you weren't the butt of his jokes and mischief . . .

No matter the prank, Hermes always seemed to get away with it. When he stole cattle from the mighty musical god, Apollo, for example, it looked like Hermes was in BIG trouble. But then he

gifted Apollo a lyre (a stringed musical instrument), and escaped unharmed.

This trickster god always wore a helmet and sandals, both with wings. If you were lucky he might lend you his sandals, which could make you fly faster than the wind. *Whooooosh!*

Hermes' work as a messenger for the other Greek gods meant that he was always on the move. He could travel to the human realm where he had fun pranking people but also invented the alphabet, dice, pan pipes and mathematics – all jolly useful.

So, you've read about these five magical mythical figures, which one do you think is top god?

WOULD YOU RATHER

weave and babysit as an Athenian woman

OR wrestle and race as a Spartan woman?

A LOT OF OUR INFORMATION ABOUT ANCIENT GREECE IS PACKED WITH MEN, MEN, MEN, MOSTLY BECAUSE THE HISTORIANS OF THE TIME WERE MEN, WHO DIDN'T CARE ALL THAT MUCH ABOUT WOMEN'S LIVES. MEAN. WHAT WE DO KNOW, THOUGH, IS THAT LIFE COULD LOOK VERY DIFFERENT FOR WOMEN DEPENDING ON WHICH CITY-STATE THEY LIVED IN.

Athenian woman

Do you like the sound of a quiet life at home? Athenian women certainly got that – but it came with some downsides.

In Athens, women were definitely seen as coming second to men. They couldn't own land or houses, vote, fight in armies or do any juicy jobs such as being an architect or tyrant. Most Athenian girls didn't even go to school and were usually married by 15.

As an Athenian woman, you'd stay at home almost all the time, looking after children, weaving, doing the cleaning, washing and cooking (with the help of slaves if you were wealthy). You'd only go out for ceremonies like funerals and some festivals (see page 33). Wealthier women weren't even allowed to go shopping and sent their slaves out to do it for them!

Bonus fact

A few resourceful Greek women broke the traditional mould. Sappho of Lesbos and Telesilla of Argos became famous poets, and Arete of Cyrene (a Greek colony in Libya) was a philosopher.

Spartan woman

Did you choose an action-packed life?

Unlike many other city-states, girls
in Sparta often got an education. This
included a lot of PE . . . Sparta was BIG
on sport and exercise. They thought
that if women were to become mothers,

they should be fit and strong. Spartan women could expect to practise running, wrestling and maybe even other sports, such as javelin.

They could also own land and property, and took charge of running the family farm or other business if their husband went off to war (which happened fairly often).

Many Spartan women had helots to help them around the house with cleaning and cooking – go back to page 23 to read about them.

All that exercising could really build an appetite. If you're ready for a Greek snack, turn to the next page . . .

GREEK EXTRAS
Greek grub

The Greeks ate two or three meals a day starting with a basic breakfast of flatbread, often dipped in wine with perhaps a few figs or olives. No cornflakes or beans on toast. Soz.

As an ordinary Greek, your other meals would include plenty of barley porridge, lentils, peas and beans. As a result, you'd be very gassy . . . farts ahoy! What would you choose from this ancient Greek menu?

Pelican pie
MOST ANCIENT GREEKS RARELY ATE RED MEAT BUT DID CHOMP DOWN ON BIRDS, SUCH AS SPARROWS, THRUSHES, SWANS AND PELICANS.

Kykeon

HOW ABOUT A DRINK TO WASH DOWN
YOUR STRINGY SPARROW? KYKEON
WAS THE WORLD'S FIRST SMOOTHIE,
BUT DON'T GET YOUR HOPES UP.
IT WAS A SLUDGY MIX OF BARLEY,
WATER, HERBS AND GOAT'S CHEESE.

Echinous

SOME ANCIENT GREEKS SWORE BY SCOFFING
SEA URCHINS. THESE SPIKY SEA CREATURES
WERE CAUGHT BY HAND (OUCH!), COVERED
IN MUD, THEN BAKED.

Black soup

THIS SPARTAN BROTH WAS MADE OF
BOILED PIGS' LEGS AND PLENTY OF
PIGS' BLOOD. THE ONLY FLAVOURINGS
IN IT WERE SALT AND VINEGAR, THE
LATTER TO STOP ALL THE BLOOD IN THE
SOUP FROM CLOTTING!

WOULD YOU RATHER

make a living by scraping sweat off stinky athletes

OR by stealing cabbages?

FIRST THINGS FIRST, IF YOU WEREN'T FILTHY RICH, OR
A PEASANT WHO LIVED OFF THE LAND, YOU'D NEED
TO FIND A JOB TO GET MONEY FOR YOUR FOOD. WELL,
THERE WAS ONE OTHER OPTION: RESORTING TO A LIFE
OF CRIME, PILFERING YOUR MEALS. BUT THIS COULD
HAVE NASTY CONSEQUENCES ...

Scrape sweat off athletes

Did you choose the law-abiding but smelly option? Hold your nose . . .

In ancient Greece, being muscly and sporty was a BIG plus. Being a successful athlete would earn you major respect, but there's no success without hard work. Athletes needed to train, and they needed people to help them do it.

In many Greek city-states, athletes trained at a *gymnasion* (gymnasium), helped by trainers called *paidotribes**. As a trainer, you'd need wrists of iron and strong fingers too. Your main job before training was to massage your champion with olive oil. If the athlete was a hefty

* No women were allowed – tough luck for sporty girls.

wrestler or discus thrower, there'd be a lot of muscle to massage!

Worse was to come. The ancient Greeks didn't have soap, so the olive oil would become mixed with dirt and lots of stinky sweat. The *paidotribes'* job was to get the athlete clean by scraping it all off using a blade called a *strigil*.

The gunky, stinky mix of oil, sweat and dirt was called *gloios*. Trainers would carefully collect it and pour it into bottles or jars. Why? Because *gloios* was sold as a medicine – some people thought it helped relieve aches and pains!

Stealing cabbages

Did you choose a life of crime? Think that stealing food would be better than sweat-scraping for a living?

Think again. Thieves rarely lived happy lives in ancient Greece, especially in Athens during the reign of Draco, an early ruler. Around 621BCE, Draco laid down Athens' first set of written laws and they were BRUTAL.

He was keen on the death penalty, both for horrid crimes like murder, and for stealing one measly apple or cabbage. *Gulp*! It wasn't much comfort that a thief could choose was the way they died. There were three common endings:

1. BEING THROWN OFF A CLIFF OR DOWN A DEEP PIT. IF THE FALL DIDN'T KILL YOU STONE DEAD, BEING STUCK THERE, IN AGONY, WITH NO HOPE OF RESCUE, MIGHT.

2. BEING TIED TO A HEAVY WOODEN BOARD AND LEFT IN THE COUNTRY TO DIE. YOU COULDN'T WALK OR FEND OFF WILD CREATURES. YOU'D GET HUNGRY, BUT NOT AS HUNGRY AS THE WILD WOLVES WHO MIGHT DECIDE YOU WERE DINNER ...

3. BEING GIVEN POISON, SUCH AS HEMLOCK, TO DRINK. THIS IS HOW THE LIFE OF PHILOSOPHER SOCRATES ENDED. QUICKER THAN OPTION 2, BUT STILL REALLY UNPLEASANT ... AND JUST AS FINAL.

Death for stealing vegetables? Bottling up athletes' sweat? What a strange world some ancient Greeks lived in. Take your time to make your decision, go and *veg out* if you want. No *sweat*.

GREEK EXTRAS
Jobs board

What brilliant skills do you have? Have a look at these ancient Greek jobs – can you find one that you think you would have been good at?

ORACLE

ARE YOU A WOMAN? CAN YOU TALK TO THE GODS AND DISPENSE ADVICE TO HUMANS? BECOME AN ORACLE TODAY!

PERKS:
- Respect for your mega skills! This rare type of priestess was thought to be able to talk directly to the gods. The word of an oracle was never doubted (even though most of their prophecies were quite vague).
- Fame (especially if you worked at the Temple of Apollo in Delphi). Important figures would rely on you to make big decisions.
- Spa access – in between doling out predictions, you'd bathe in holy pools of water to purify yourself.

BE PREPARED FOR:
- Being busy! People would flock to the temples you worked at, to hear your precious words of wisdom.

ARCHITECT
ARE YOU MAGIC AT MATHS? DO YOU KNOW YOUR MARBLE FROM YOUR LIMESTONE? COME AND BE A *ROCK STAR* AND BUILD BIG!

PERKS:
- Good for perfectionists with an eye for art. Most Greeks liked their buildings in perfect proportion. For example, some types of column had to be precisely nine times higher than the width of their base.
- You'd get really good at drawing and maths.
- Potential to work on some iconic buildings.

BE PREPARED FOR:
- Working without any computers to help design projects.
- Not making any mistakes! You needed to be precise and perfect as your employers could be spending a fortune. The Parthenon (a temple in Athens dedicated to the goddess Athena) cost more than a fleet of 00 warships!

CRAFT WORKER
GOOD WITH YOUR HANDS? BECOME A CRAFT WORKER. SLAVES CAN APPLY!

PERKS:
- Decent pay – about as much as a hoplite soldier, without the risk of death.
- Potential for making friends in the workshop.
- Bonus points from Hephaestus, the god of craft (just remember to pray!).

BE PREPARED FOR:
- Spending long, repetitive days practising your craft.

PRIEST OR PRIESTESS
GREAT WITH GODS AND GUTS? BE A PRIEST! MEN AND WOMEN ACCEPTED.

PERKS:
- Comes with a temple and plenty of free meat from offerings.

BE PREPARED FOR:
- Doing a lot of cleaning. Your job would be keeping those temples spotless!
- Spending a lot of time up to your elbows in guts and gore after a sacrifice.

OR battle on water as a trireme sailor?

ALL THE GREEK CITY-STATES HAD ARMIES AND SOME HAD NAVIES AS WELL. WHERE DID THE GREEKS KEEP THEIR ARMIES? UP THEIR SLEEVIES, OF COURSE! NO, SERIOUSLY, THEY LIVED IN BARRACKS OR IN TOWNS WITH THEIR FAMILIES, AND WERE TREATED PRETTY WELL, UNTIL THEY HAD TO GO TO WAR ... WHICH COULD BE A CHALLENGE, ON LAND OR SEA!

Battle on foot

Think you'd rather stick to dry land?
Put on your armour and hop to it!

Hoplites were named after the *hoplon* –
a round, wooden shield covered in bronze
that each soldier carried. They might
be called hoplites, but these warriors
wouldn't be hopping very lightly – the
hoplon weighed up to 12kg (the same as
about three pet cats). Mind you, the *hoplon*
did give good protection and could be
personalised with symbols relating to your
family or where you came from.

Once they were all kitted up, hoplites
were ready to march onto the battlefield,
huddled up in a tight formation called

a *phalanx* (this would likely be very whiffy – no deodorant in ancient Greece!). You'd stand shoulder to stinky shoulder with your fellow hoplites with your shields overlapping to protect the whole *phalanx* from arrows and spears.

The *phalanx* would march forward and force through enemy ranks, where they'd use razor-sharp swords, spears and their mighty shields to duff up opponents. Be careful – stragglers could be picked off by the enemy!

Battle on water

What about a life on the open ocean?
Sounds *oarsome*? Let's set sail!

Greek sailors would head out to war
on board a huge warship called a *trireme*.
These vessels were around 35m long,
sleek, fast and deadly to rival boats.

Trireme meant 'three rows'. Every ship had three banks of oars stacked on top of each other on both sides. Back and forth you (along with around 170 others) would row, all day, every day. In battle, your ship's captain might order you to row even faster, so that your ship would crunch into an enemy vessel and sink it.

But it wasn't all plain sailing. Similar tactics could be used on YOUR *trireme* and there was always the threat of flaming arrows setting your wooden ship alight. If enemy attacks didn't get you, the unpredictable and sometimes stormy seas might. Hope you're a strong swimmer!

So what will it be, fighting on land or battling at sea? For more battles and bashing, turn the page . . .

GREEK EXTRAS
Top thumps

Greek armies and navies fought some epic conflicts against each other and outsiders, such as the Persians (who lived around the area of modern-day Iran).

The Battle of Marathon: 490BCE
Result: Athens wins!

The Persians invaded Greece from the east and were closing in on Athens. The city's ten generals decided to attack using next to no soldiers on horses. They hoped their hoplites (see page 64) would do the job. And they did!

A messenger called Pheidippides sprinted from Marathon to Athens,

a distance of about 40km, to bring the news of victory, then dropped down dead from exhaustion. Oops. This is where we get the name of the marathon long distance running race.

The Siege of Rhodes: 305-304BCE
Result: Draw!

Rhodes forged a close alliance with Egypt . . . and Demetrius, a Macedonian military leader, didn't like it. His army and navy, plus fleets of pirate ships, laid siege to the city for over a year.

Demetrius' army built a gigantic siege tower out of wood covered in metal plates. It was called a *helepolis*, stood 40m high and loomed over Rhodes' walls.

The terrible armoured tower contained huge catapults which could fire rocks weighing 80kg, and was said to take around 3,000 men to move it into place.

Even with the *helepolis*, Demetrius could not break through. Every time part of Rhodes' walls came tumbling down, the city's people managed to defend them. In the end, an agreement was reached, the siege ended and the *helepolis* was abandoned.

Demetrius and his army had left most of their equipment behind, and the people of Rhodes made the most of things, and sold it. They used the profit to build a giant gold statue – the Colossus of Rhodes – to commemorate the heroic defence of their city.

WOULD YOU RATHER

heal the sick like Hippocrates

OR be a maths whizz like Archimedes?

ANCIENT GREECE WAS FULL OF A-LIST STARS, FROM GREAT PHILOSOPHERS TO ARCHITECTS, POETS AND HISTORIANS. THEIR BRILLIANT BRAINS DEVELOPED IDEAS THAT WE STILL USE TODAY. IF YOU ARE WOKEN UP BY AN ALARM CLOCK, YOU ARE USING A DESCENDENT OF AN ANCIENT GREEK INVENTION! BEWARE THOUGH, THEY MAY HAVE BEEN BRAINY, BUT SOME OF THEM HAD UNUSUAL METHODS ...

Heal the sick

It's a bold choice you've made – hope you're not bothered by blood . . . or worse!

Born on the island of Kos in 460BCE, Hippocrates was one of the first physicians to study illnesses scientifically. Well, sort of. In early ancient Greece, most people thought gods or spirits were responsible for illness and disease. Hippocrates thought there were natural causes behind bad health and was the first to properly examine his patients.

Hippocrates was a thorough guy. He thought nothing of giving his patients' sweat, spit and wee a good sniff to see if he could detect something wrong.

For headaches, he would stick his finger in the patient's ear, pull out some earwax and eat it, checking the taste. *Mmmm.* For other ailments, he might smell, taste or even *eat* a sample of patient's poo, snot, vomit or pus from a wound. *Yuck!*

Hippocrates got a lot right though. He often prescribed changes of diet and exercise to patients. He was the first to use terms like 'epidemic' and 'relapse', and insisted the new medics that he trained kept patient records.

Be a maths whizz

Would you like to wrap your head around some tricky sums? Meet maths-extraordinaire, Archimedes!

Archimedes was born in the Greek city-state of Syracuse in 287BCE, and was a bit of a maths genius. You'd spy him around town, deep in thought, as he wrestled with yet another tricky problem. His most famous discovery was how to measure the volume of an odd-shaped object by seeing how much water it pushed away (displaced) when lowered into a tub.

Archimedes was in the bath at the time of this revelation. He is said to have leapt out, cried *"Eureka!"* meaning, "I found it!" and then streaked down the street, completely naked – such was his joy at his *nude* – sorry, *new* – discovery.

Archimedes was also magic with machines. He was the first to fully understand how levers worked and used them to build war machines. He is even said to have invented a DEATH RAY which focused sunlight into a beam that could set enemy ships alight*.

*This might have been big talk from our maths man – we have no proof it was built!

EUREKA!

Turn the page to meet some more ancient Greek cleverclogs!

Top thinkers hall of fame

The ancient Greeks were a seriously brainy bunch. They were amongst the first people in the west to really *think about thinking* (philosophy), contemplating what people and the world are all about. One Greek scholar called Plato opened the first school for philosophers in Athens in 387BCE, where he had hundreds of students. Read about these fab four philosophers, and think for yourself – who would you rather go back in time to meet?

Thales of Miletus

Born: Around 624BCE

Said: "The greatest [thing] is space; for it holds all things."

One of the very first Greek philosophers we know about, Thales was the first person to predict a solar eclipse (when the Moon blocks out all light from the Sun) and described many rules in geometry. He also learned how to measure the heights of things just by using angles and the lengths of the shadows they cast. Clever boy.

Not so clever ...

Thales believed the Earth floated on a giant sea of water.

Just hold still, Rover ...

Pythagoras of Samos

Born: Around 570BCE

Said: "Number rules the Universe."

Pythagoras was the first to use maths to describe and explain the world. He discovered rules about triangles and ratios, was one of the first to suggest Earth was ball-shaped rather than flat, and used maths to explain music. His followers – the Pythagoreans – were a secret cult with strange rules including always putting on their right sandal first and never going for a wee whilst facing the Sun!

Not so clever . . .

Pythagoras believed that beans had souls and should never be eaten. No beans on toast for him.

Socrates

Born: Around 470BCE

Said: "I cannot teach anybody anything. I can only make them think."

After serving as a hoplite in Athens' army (see page 64), Socrates invented new ways to think about the world. He believed that knowledge led to happiness and used all of Athens as his classroom, wandering the streets to talk with people, quizzing people about the meaning of things, such as fairness.

He upset the rulers of Athens so much that he was sentenced to death at the age of 70. He drank a cup of poisonous hemlock (a type of plant).

Not so clever ... or the cleverest?

One of Socrates' main beliefs was that he knew absolutely nothing at all. It might have been modesty, or even a cunning way to start conversations – or maybe it was a clever way to learn, by going into subjects with an open mind.

Aristotle of Stagira

Born: 384BCE

Said: "Knowing yourself is the beginning of all wisdom."

This big thinker studied everything, from how the weather works to the insides of animals he cut up. He was the first to classify living things into different groups, and invented types of logical reasoning to work out facts. He was also personal tutor to Alexander the Great, who went on to be a hugely successful leader and soldier. Aristotle's work has influenced thinking in Europe for over 2,000 years – not too shabby!

Not so clever . . .

Aristotle believed that eels didn't reproduce, they just appeared out of mud.

Which of these brainy Greeks would you rather meet?

WOULD YOU RATHER

play an ancient Greek ball game

OR give your friend a piggyback ride?

YOU DIDN'T HAVE TO BE A TOP OLYMPIC ATHLETE TO PLAY SPORTS AND GAMES IN ANCIENT GREECE. KIDS AND ADULTS WOULD RUN ABOUT, HAVING FUN IN THE MEDITERRANEAN SUNSHINE. DEPENDING ON WHERE YOU WERE, SOME GAMES COULD GET PRETTY ROUGH ...

Play a ball game

Uh oh – you've chosen a scary game!
Grab your boots and get ready for
a kick-about, ancient Greek style.

OK, the ancient Greeks didn't
invent football as we know it
today – but, they did play
a game called
episkyros. To
play, two teams
of around 12-14
would gather on a
pitch with three
lines on it. One

line went down the middle of the pitch, between the two teams, the other two lines ran behind each team. Each team would pass the ball around the pitch, aiming to get the opposing team to go behind their line – a bit like modern-day rugby.

This was a game that could get seriously physical – especially if you played in Sparta. And remember, no shin pads or helmets!

Give your friend a piggyback

If you'd rather play a game with a smaller team, you've chosen well – welcome to *ephedrismos*! Here's how to play this popular ancient Greek game:

STEP 1

FIND A FRIEND TO PLAY WITH.

STEP 2

FETCH A STONE THAT CAN BE KNOCKED OVER, AND STAND IT ON THE GROUND.

STEP 3

TAKE IT IN TURNS TO THROW ANOTHER STONE FROM THE SAME DISTANCE, AND TRY TO KNOCK OVER THE FIRST STONE. WHOEVER DOES THIS IS THE WINNER.

STEP 4

THE LOSER HAS TO GIVE THE WINNER A PIGGYBACK WHILE BLINDFOLDED.

STEP 5

THE LOSER TRIES TO TOUCH THE KNOCKED-OVER STONE.

This game was popular with ancient Greek girls – many statues from the period show girls and young women playing the game together.

GREEK EXTRAS
It's all Greek to me

Shhhhh. Can you keep a secret? This could be vital in ancient Greek times – be it news of a hush-hush trading deal or orders for an army to attack.

Some ancient Greeks, such as the Spartans, made use of simple secret code systems. One of the most common was the *scytale*. This was a long strip of parchment or other material wound multiple times around a wooden rod or cylinder, with a message written on it.

When taken off the rod, the message would be hidden or worn and carried by a messenger. Even if it was discovered, it would make no sense . . . until it was

wrapped again around the same width rod or cylinder to decode it.

1. FIND A LONG, THIN STRIP OF PAPER. TAPE ONE END OF THE STRIP TO ONE END OF THE INSIDE TUBE OF A KITCHEN ROLL.

2. WIND THE PAPER AROUND THE ROLL IN A COIL SO THAT THE EDGES OF THE PAPER STRIP MEET (OR JUST OVERLAP A TINY BIT).

3. WHEN THE PAPER IS FULLY WOUND, WRITE YOUR MESSAGE ONTO THE PAPER, ALONG THE LENGTH OF THE CYLINDER (LIKE IN THE PICTURE BELOW).

4. UNWIND THE PAPER. NOW TRY TO READ IT. DOES IT LOOK ALL JUMBLED UP? GREAT! YOU HAVE YOUR SECRET MESSAGE.

5. GIVE IT TO SOMEONE ELSE. THEY CAN DECODE THE MESSAGE BY WINDING THE PAPER AROUND THEIR OWN KITCHEN ROLL TUBE (JUST MAKE SURE THE TUBE IS THE SAME SIZE AS YOURS).

WOULD YOU RATHER

visit an ancient Greek doctor

OR take your chances in a pankration wrestling match?

ANCIENT GREECE MIGHT HAVE BEEN FULL OF CLEVER IDEAS AND GREAT STORIES, BUT EVERYDAY LIFE SOMETIMES GOT PAINFUL, ESPECIALLY IF YOU WERE UNLUCKY ENOUGH TO GET ILL OR INJURED. SPEAKING OF INJURY ... SOME GREEKS TOOK PART IN COMPETITIONS THAT WERE VERY LIKELY TO LEAD TO BUMPS AND BRUISES, IF NOT WORSE!

Visit a doctor

Welcome to the waiting room – the ancient Greek doctor will see you shortly. Hope you're ready!

In the first centuries of their civilization, the Greeks were extremely superstitious and believed sickness could only be cured with help from gods. Some Greeks carried around small pieces of lucky bone to protect them from diseases.

It's no shocker that they flocked to temples called *asclepions*, dedicated to the god of healing, Asclepius. There, priests might have chanted a bit for you and made offerings to the gods. They may also have given sick people a drink containing ground-up plants. This might even have helped . . . The ancient Greeks sometimes ground up the bark of willow trees – more than 2,000 years later, people realised this bark contains a natural painkiller called salicylic acid, the basis of aspirin tablets!

You could set up as an ancient Greek physician with next to no training. You just needed patients who believed in your abilities to heal them. Some physicians did learn to set broken bones so they healed well. But others had some truly rotten remedies . . .

If you had a painful slipped disc (when tissue in your spine is pushed out of place), doctors might lie you on the ground then jump up and down on your back. *Owwww!*

One cutting-edge cure for fevers and other illnesses was bloodletting. It was thought that your body could build up too much blood, which would cause health problems. The physician would slice a cut into your arm or leg and let plenty of blood flow out.

All of these horrible treatments were nothing compared to surgery though. This was used as a last resort when all other remedies had failed. The problem was the PAIN. There were no anaesthetics to put you to sleep nor super-clean surgery tools. Greek surgeons used their bronze knives and saws, while the was patient wide awake and in agony. *Ouch, ouch, OUCH!*

Take your chances in pankration

Have you ever tried judo, karate, or another martial art? In ancient Greece, things were a lot more brutal – especially the pankration, a truly no-holds barred punch-up that became a sport at the ancient Olympic games in 648BCE. pankration was (more or less) a combination of wrestling and boxing. Read the scroll across the page for a rough idea of the rules . . .

You won your bout when your opponent was knocked out cold or gave up. Three-time champion Sostratos of Sicyon's signature move was to bend and break the fingers of his opponents. SNAP! He did this finger by finger until they gave up. *Owwwwww!*

1. NO BITING.

2. NO GOUGING OF THE EYES.

3. PUNCHES OR KICKS TO THE GROIN ARE A NO.

4. IF RULES 1, 2 OR 3 ARE BROKEN, THE COMPETITOR CAN EXPECT TO GET HIT WITH A STICK OR WHIP WIELDED BY A REFEREE.

5. ER, THAT'S ABOUT IT.

With all the wrestling the ancient Greeks did (whether with illness or each other) death was fairly common. But what happened when people did die? Turn the page to find out . . .

GREEK EXTRAS

Funerals and the Underworld

When an ancient Greek person died, rituals would take place to prepare them for the Underworld. Women would wash and prepare the body, and might even cut their own hair short to show their grief. More mourning would take place on the way to the burial, usually in cemeteries outside the city walls, with mourners crying, wailing and moaning.

The Greeks believed that the journey to the Underworld included crossing the mythical river Styx. A ferryman called Charon would take the dead across the river for a fee. So, a dead person would be buried with a coin underneath their tongue to pay for the crossing.

When they got to the Underworld, the deceased would be in the territory of Hades, god of the dead. Hades was the original goth – he had a chariot drawn by black horses, a helmet that made the wearer invisible and he liked things dark and gloomy. His closest companion was a horrible hound with three heads called Cerberus. G-g-good doggy! Greeks above ground were often too scared to mention him by name!

OR stay at home as a market trader?

THERE WAS A LOT OF BUYING AND SELLING IN ANCIENT GREECE. FOODS, CLOTH, JEWELLERY AND PEOPLE ALL COULD BE TRADED. THERE WAS NO INTERNET BUT YOU COULD ORDER A MERCHANT SHIP FULL OF GRAIN OR SILVER FOR DELIVERY WEEKS LATER. OR, IN MOST GREEK TOWNS AND CITIES, YOU COULD BUY FAR SMALLER QUANTITIES FROM TRADERS AT MARKETS. DON'T FORGET YOUR WALLET!

Travel as a merchant

Do you like risks and gambles? Are you good with numbers and making quick decisions? Can you haggle? Do you like travel and want to get rich? If you answered yes, yes, yes and YES, a merchant's life might have been for you.

Trade was absolutely vital to city-states. Few had enough land to grow the great variety of food that their inhabitants wanted. It was better to specialise in a few things and buy in others from places near and far.

Greek city-states traded between themselves but also with places all around the Mediterranean. As a merchant, you'd try to fulfil the city-states' shopping lists by ferrying cargoes of goods, food or materials from place to place. The aim was to buy cheap and sell expensive – making a big, juicy profit in each port you arrived at. But it didn't always work out that way.

For starters, you probably had a single ship and not enough money to buy an entire cargo to fill it AND pay your crew. So, you had to borrow from money-lenders. They might ask for double their money back – even if you only borrowed the money for a few weeks. What a rip-off.

CORINTH
Pottery

CYRENE
Grain & veg

SICILY
Wool

CYPRUS
Timber

SYRIA
Spices

CARTHAGE
Textiles

Then, there were the suppliers you bought your goods from. They could drive a hard bargain, or raise the price of their goods. Even worse, they could be absolute cheats.

You then had to get your cargo home safely . . . not as easy as it sounds. Your ship could be tossed and turned by sudden storms or spring a leak or two and sink. Or you could be attacked by fierce pirates who would steal your cargo. Either way, you'd be ruined.

And there was always the danger that the cargo you had staked all your wealth on was no longer in fashion by the time you got it back to port . . . or another pesky merchant had got there before you.

Prefer to stay a little closer to home? It could be an exciting life – but get ready for some hard work!

You'd need to be up at dawn, haggling furiously with merchants or farmers to buy goods. Whatever you bought, you'd try to flog for a higher price at an *agora*.

What's an *agora*, you say? These open areas or squares were found in the centre of most ancient Greek towns. As a trader you'd have to stick your elbows out and jostle to get a top selling spot.

Some traders were shady – they might sell rotting goods hidden by placing fresh ones on top, or weigh items on bent scales so they sold the customer less than they paid for. To cut this sort of stuff out, most cities employed officials called *metronomoi*, who strode around keeping a close eye on traders. If you were caught cheating customers, expect to be fined or even given a whipping!

What would you put on your ancient Greek shopping list?

GREEK EXTRAS
Toilets

You may be wondering . . . philosophy, maths and clever inventions are all very well, but what did the ancient Greeks do when they needed to go to the loo?

Well, Greek toilets were as clever as the rest of their developments. In fact, they invented what may well have been the very first flushing toilet!

This *poo*-seful invention was installed in the Palace at Knossos, on the island of Crete. This island was home to the Minoans, who formed one of the first civilizations in Europe. Impressive stuff! The palace itself was built around 1900BCE – nearly 2,000 years before the

Romans built the Colosseum in Rome.

The toilet in Knossos was attached
to a special channel – when it had been
used, the visitor poured water into it, and
whatever was in there would be flushed
down the channel. Easy *pee*-sy.

OR battle an angry cyclops and sneaky sirens?

HEROES IN ANCIENT GREEK MYTHOLOGY COULD USUALLY BE FOUND OUT ON AN EPIC QUEST. WHETHER THEY WERE BATTLING SEA MONSTERS, FIGHTING WARS OR ARGUING WITH GODS, THEY HAD FEW QUIET MOMENTS. TWO FAMOUS GREEK HEROES, HERACLES AND ODYSSEUS, WERE BUSIER THAN MOST, AND SPENT YEARS FIGHTING MONSTERS AND COMPLETING TASKS SENT BY THE GODS TO ANNOY THEM.

Battle a lion, dog and snake

If you're great with animals and have a sense of adventure, great choice! Meet the mighty Heracles . . .

Heracles (also known as Hercules) was half-god, half-human. Zeus, king of the gods, was his dad. Wow!

Unfortunately, Zeus' wife Hera had it in for Hercules because his mother was another woman. She made Heracles mad, causing him to kill his own wife and children. When he came to his senses, Heracles was terribly upset and sought forgiveness. As his punishment, he was told to serve a king called Eurystheus who set him 12 seemingly impossible tasks.

Impossible, you say? Not for our hero. These tasks, known as the Labours of Heracles, featured a lot of journeying, wrestling, and killing (Greek myths were often pretty bloodthirsty). Poor Heracles must have been exhausted, especially as many of the tasks required fighting monsters and other far-from-friendly foes.

1. SLAY THE GIANT, FIERCE NEMEAN LION

← My arrows bounced off it, I had to wrestle it to death.

2. KILL THE LERNAEAN HYDRA

← A serpent with nine heads. Nasty!

3. CAPTURE THE CERYNEIAN HIND

← This deer was so fast, it took me a year to catch her.

4. CAPTURE THE ERYMANTHIAN BOAR

← This was epic. I had to fight centaurs, too!

5. CLEAN THE HUGE STABLES OF KING AUGEAS IN A SINGLE DAY

↑ Super stinky!

6. DEFEAT THE MAN-EATING STYMPHALIAN BIRDS

↖ Scary – they had poisonous poo.

7. CAPTURE THE CRETAN BULL

8. STEAL THE MARES (FEMALE HORSES) OF DIOMEDES

9. STEAL THE BELT OF HIPPOLYTE, FIERCE QUEEN OF THE AMAZONS

← I had to sail the seas and fight a whole army . . . just for a belt. Sheesh!

10. STEAL THE CATTLE OF THE GIANT, GERYON

← Cow am I doing?

11. STEAL APPLES FROM THE GARDENS OF THE HESPERIDES

↑ I had to roam through Africa, Asia and fight gods just to get there.

12. BRING BACK THE THREE-HEADED DOG CERBERUS FROM THE UNDERWORLD (SEE PAGE 104).

↑ Phew! Finished.

It wasn't all bulging biceps and epic strength, though. Heracles also had to exercise his brain. Cleaning King Augeas' stables for example was an impossible job until he built a dam to divert a river to wash the stables' vast mountains of stinky muck away. Clever.

There's got to be an easier way...

Battle a cyclops and sirens

If a trip out to sea sounds like more your scene, meet Odysseus – cunning plotter, and sailor extraordinaire!

Odysseus was the main hero of one of the oldest stories from ancient Greece, Homer's *Odyssey*. It follows his journey home from the Trojan war – a trip that took him ten years. On his way, Odysseus had to get out of some sticky situations. When he and his crew got trapped in a cave belonging to

a cyclops (a one-eyed giant), they made a hasty getaway by clinging to the underside of some sheep. His crew also had to sail past the sirens, deadly creatures with voices so beautiful that sailors couldn't resist sailing towards them, where they would drown in dangerous water. Odysseus wanted to hear the singing, so got his men to tie him to the ship's mast so he could safely listen to them. He had his cake . . . and ate it!

Are you feeling heroic? Which challenge would you take?

GREEK EXTRAS
Heroes

Greek legends contained hundreds of heroes. Here are just a few ...

Atalanta – this heroine loved the wilderness. As a baby, she was cared for by a bear! Later in life, she said she'd only marry a suitor who could outrun her in a race. She beat everyone apart from one suitor, who got the goddess Aphrodite to help him cheat!

Achilles – the greatest Greek warrior. He did have one weakness though: his heel. When he was a baby, his mother had

dipped him in a magical river
to make him invincible,
but she held him by the
heel to do so, leaving it
unprotected. Oops!

Penelope – the very patient
wife of Odysseus. She was mobbed
by suitors while her husband was away,
and held them off by saying she needed
to finish her weaving – while sneakily
unpicking her work every night.

Orpheus – this musical hero attempted
to rescue his girlfriend Eurydice from the
Underworld. Hades agreed, saying she
could follow him out as long as he didn't
look back. He did – and back she went.

WOULD YOU RATHER

be able to turn people to stone like Medusa

OR turn people into pigs like Circe?

ZEUS, POSEIDON AND THE OTHER OLYMPIAN GODS HAD SOME POWERFUL SKILLS, AND YOU DEFINITELY WOULDN'T WANT TO CATCH THEM ON A BAD DAY ... BUT THEY WEREN'T THE ONLY ONES WHO COULD PACK A PUNCH! GREEK LEGENDS ARE CHOC FULL OF STORIES OF HEROES GETTING ON THE WRONG SIDE OF POWERFUL BEINGS, INCLUDING MEDUSA AND CIRCE ...

Turn people to stone

Do you like statues? Dislike interfering gods? Welcome to the world of one of Greece's most misunderstood women . . .

Medusa was a pretty woman – so pretty that the god, Poseidon fancied her rotten. This angered the goddess Athena who, in a flash, turned Medusa's skin green and her hair into live snakes whose fangs were full of venom. Bit of a harsh reaction!

Medusa also possessed a scary superpower – one

look from her was enough to turn you into stone . . . forever. Yikes!

Eventually, a young man called Perseus was sent by a Greek king to bump Medusa off. To avoid becoming a lovely piece of sculpture, he was armed with a big mirror on his shield so he didn't have to look at her directly. Sneaky . . . Perseus chopped off Medusa's head and used it as a weapon to turn others into stone. Eventually, he gave it as a present to the goddess Athena, who had helped him along the way.

Turn people into pigs

Does a farmyard life sound *oink*-redible to you? Welcome to the island of Aeaea (pronounced ay-ee-yah), home of the mysterious sorceress Circe . . .

Remember Odysseus from page 122? One day on his journey, he found himself on Aeaea with his crew. Circe was not in the mood to hang out with a bunch of sailors, so promptly turned them all into pigs by placing magical

That's snort fair!

drugs into their food. Or, she tried to. Odysseus was notoriously sneaky and had some powerful god friends. He had been given a special herb by the god Hermes, that protected him from this piggy trick. You could say it *saved his bacon* . . . In any case, Odysseus made Circe change all his crew back into people – they then all spent a merry year staying on the island with her!

What magical superpower would you choose?

GREEK EXTRAS
Way to go

According to ancient accounts, some Greeks died seriously strange deaths . . .

Milo of Croton

Give a big cheer for Milo – six-time ancient Olympic wrestling champion and the most famous athlete of his day.

One day, he spotted a tree in a forest that was partly split in two, and couldn't resist testing his strength. He tried to rip the trunk in two with his bare hands.

Tree-mendous mistake. His hands got stuck in the crack and he could not get them free. Later, a pack of wolves made a meal of Milo!

Aeschylus

This celebrated Greek playwright was the first known writer of Greek tragedies – plays that didn't end well for one  or some of the main characters. Around 455BCE, he was said to have been sitting in a field in Gela, Sicily, when an eagle dropped a tortoise it had caught straight onto his head. The eagle had mistaken Aeschylus's bald bonce for a rock! The blow from the tortoise's hard shell killed him instantly.

Heraclitus

This philosopher suffered from edema, a condition where the body retains too much water. As a cure, he decided to bury himself under a mountain of warm cow dung which he thought would draw the excess water out of his body. It didn't work. The cow dung dried, hardened and trapped him in place, and allegedly he was then eaten by wild dogs.

What a *ruff* way to go.

Just one more cow pat...

Empedocles

Born around 490BCE in Sicily, Empedocles developed a reputation as a bit of a genius – in poetry, public speaking and thinking in general.

However, all the praise went to his head, and he started believing that he was a god. To prove it to his followers, he clambered up the slopes of Mount Etna – a live, active volcano – and jumped into the boiling crater. He was convinced he would survive and return a true god. He didn't!

How it all ended

With there being so many city-states
in ancient Greece, conflict was fairly
common – decades of wars between
city-states in the fourth century BCE
had weakened them and left them
ripe for invasion. Enter Philip II of
Macedon, Greece's northern neighbour.
He conquered Thebes and Athens in
338BCE. When Philip died, his son,
Alexander the Great took over . . .
and built the immensely powerful
Macedonian Empire. He conquered

Greece, Egypt, the Middle East and pressed onto into Asia, defeating the Persians and reaching India.

When he died suddenly in 323BCE, a mega struggle for power saw his brief empire split into multiple mini empires. These were later conquered by Roman forces who were big fans of the Greeks. The Romans were real copycats and borrowed many Greek ideas, customs, architectural styles and even their gods. Cheeky! By doing this, they have helped keep our knowledge of the amazing Ancient Greeks alive.

Glossary

Acropolis – a fortress or guarded area at the top of a hill or high ground in a town. The best known acropolis is found in Athens and is called . . . the Acropolis!

Agora – a market place in a Greek town or city.

Amphora – a clay jar, usually with two handles, used by the ancient Greeks to hold wine or oil.

Centaur – a mythical beast which was half horse, half man.

City-state – a community with its own government which usually was made up of a large town or city and the surrounding area of farmland.

Colony – a town or area of land ruled by another country.

Fertile – when used about land, it means that the soil and conditions are good for growing crops.

Festival – a special day or occasion given over to celebration to honour a ruler, a god, a religion or a particular event.

Hoplite – a Greek foot soldier, named after the hoplon shield he carried.

Mediterranean – the name of the sea and area of land that separates southern Europe from the north coast of Africa.

Myths – stories and tales about imaginary characters and events.

Olympian – one of 12 gods in ancient Greek myths; a person who competes at an Olympic games.

Phalanx – a formation used by ancient Greek soldiers.

Philosopher – a person who studies and investigates questions about knowledge and existence.

Sacrifice – to kill a creature or offer food or other goods to honour a god.

Scytale – an object used to encode secret messages in ancient Greece.

Trireme – a type of ship used by the Ancient Greeks as a warship, with three rows of oars on each side.

Tyrant – someone who seized power of a city-state in ancient Greece.

Underworld – according to the ancient Greek myths, a place beneath the Earth's surface where the spirits of dead people travelled.

About the author

Clive Gifford has travelled through many parts of the ancient Greek world. He's seen temples in Rhodes, Crete and Attica, clambered up the Acropolis in Athens and stood, ready to race, on the start line of the track at the famous ancient Olympia stadium. Clive has written more than 200 books and has won the Royal Society, SLA and Blue Peter book awards. He lives in Manchester, UK.

About the illustrator

As a young boy, Tim Wesson was constantly doodling, finding any excuse to put pen to paper. Since turning his much loved pastime into his profession, Tim has achieved great success in the world of children's publishing, having illustrated and authored books across a variety of formats. He takes great delight in turning the world on its head and inviting children to go on the adventure with him.

Explore the rest of the series for more fascinating facts and hilarious WOULD YOU RATHER questions!